Lukas 11:1
"Here, leer ons bid"

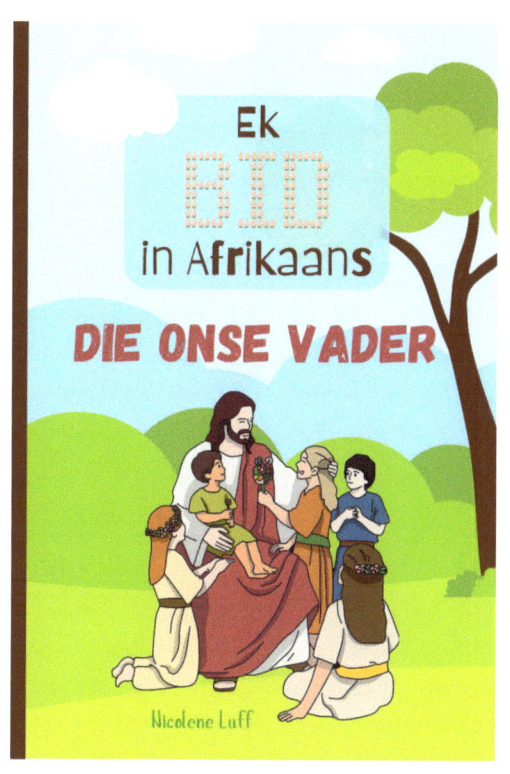

Ek BID in Afrikaans - Die Onse Vader

Copyright © 2025 by Nicolene Luff

All rights reserved.

ISBN: 979-8-9923945-5-9

Copyright © 2025 by Nicolene Luff
All rights reserved.

No part of this publication may be reproduced, distributed, or transmitted in any form or by any means, including photocopying, recording, or other electronic or mechanical methods, without the prior written permission of the publisher, except as permitted by U.S. copyright law. For permission requests, contact Nicolene Luff at nicoleneinafrikaans@gmail.com.

The story, all names, characters, and incidents portrayed in this production are fictitious. No identification with actual persons (living or deceased), places, buildings, and products is intended or should be inferred.

This publication is designed to provide accurate and authoritative information in regard to the subject matter covered. It is sold with the understanding that neither the author nor the publisher is engaged in rendering legal, investment, accounting or other professional services. While the publisher and author have used their best efforts in preparing this book, they make no representations or warranties with respect to the accuracy or completeness of the contents of this book and specifically disclaim any implied warranties of merchantability or fitness for a particular purpose. No warranty may be created or extended by sales representatives or written sales materials. The advice and strategies contained herein may not be suitable for your situation. You should consult with a professional when appropriate. Neither the publisher nor the author shall be liable for any loss of profit or any other commercial damages, including but not limited to special, incidental, consequential, personal, or other damages.

Book Cover by Nicolene Luff
Illustrations by Nicolene Luff
ISBN: 979-8-9923945-5-9

Kom ons lees

oor
Matteus 6

Jesus leer ons

hoe om

te bid

want God

weet reeds

wat

in die

hemel

woon

Laat

U Naam

geheilig

word

Laat

U

koningkryk

kom

Laat U wil geskied

soos

in die

hemel

gee ons vandag

ons daaglikse brood

net **soos** ons

vergewe,

die wat

teen **ons**

sondig

maar

verlos ons

van die

bose

want

aan U

behoort

die koninkryk

en

die krag

en die

heerlikheid

tot in

ewigheid!

AMEN

Wanneer

ons mense

vergewe

wat teen

ons sondig,

sal ons hemelse Vader ook ons sonde vergewe.

God weet hoe om vir ons te sorg,

So ons hoef oor niks te bekommer nie.

Ken jy hierdie liedjie, geskryf deur Andre du Toit?

"Lees jou Bybel, bid elke dag"

Kom ons sing saam!

"Lees jou Bybel,
bid elke dag,
bid elke dag,
bid elke dag!

Lees jou Bybel,
bid elke dag!

Want dit gee jou krag!"

This book is part of a series of books written in Afrikaans.

Ek BID in Afrikaans - Die Onse Vader
Ek BID in Afrikaans - Psalm 23
Ek BID in Afrikaans - Dankbaarheid
& more!

Be on the lookout for other Afrikaans reading & activity books!

Ek TEL in Afrikaans
Ek LEES in Afrikaans
Ek SKRYF in Afrikaans
& more!

Find them on
Amazon
&
Etsy

Let Afrikaans live on through you!

www.ingramcontent.com/pod-product-compliance
Lightning Source LLC
Chambersburg PA
CBHW041307110426
42743CB00037B/26